ESTATE PUBLICATIONS

NORWICH

ORINGLAND · WROXHAM · WYMONDHAM

C000259261

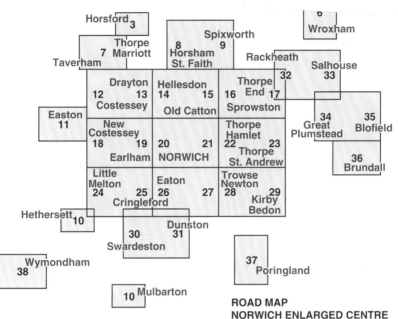

Horsford 3

Thorpe Marriott 7 8

Spixworth 9

Wroxham 6

Taverham

Horsham St. Faith

Rackheath

Salhouse

Drayton 12 13 Costessey

Hellesdon 14 15 Old Catton

Thorpe End 16 17 Sprowston

32 33

Easton 11

New Costessey 18 19 Earlham

20 21 NORWICH

Thorpe Hamlet 22 23 Thorpe St. Andrew

Great Plumstead 34

35 Blofield

Little Melton 24 25 Cringleford

Eaton 26 27

Trowse Newton 28 29 Kirby Bedon

36 Brundall

Hethersett 10

30 Swardeston

Dunston 31

37 Poringland

Wymondham 38

10 Mulbarton

ROAD MAP	Page 2
NORWICH ENLARGED CENTRE	Pages 4-5
INDEX TO STREETS	Page 39

Scale of street plans: 4 Inches to 1 Mile (unless otherwise stated)

Motorway	Stream / River
'A' Road / Dual	Canal
'B' Road / Dual	One-way Street
Minor Road / Dual	P Car Park
Track	C Public Convenience
Pedestrianized	i Tourist Information
Railway / Station	+ Place of Worship
Footpath	● Post Office

Every effort has been made to verify the accuracy of information in this book but the publishers cannot accept responsibility for expense or loss caused by an error or omission. Information that will be of assistance to the user of the maps will be welcomed.

The representation on these maps of a road, track or path is no evidence of the existence of a right of way.

Street plans prepared and published by ESTATE PUBLICATIONS, Bridewell House, TENTERDEN, KENT.
The Publishers acknowledge the co-operation of the local authorities
of towns represented in this atlas.

Ordnance Survey® This product includes mapping data licensed from Ordnance Survey® with the permission of the Controller of Her Majesty's Stationery Office.

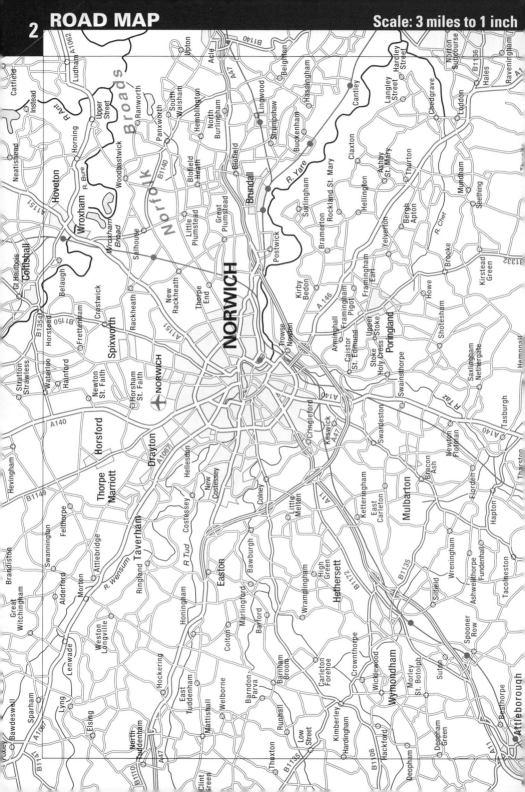

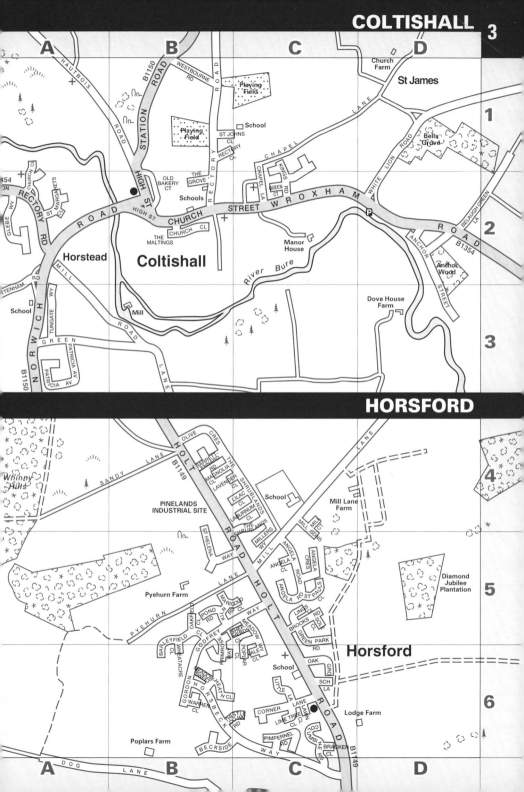

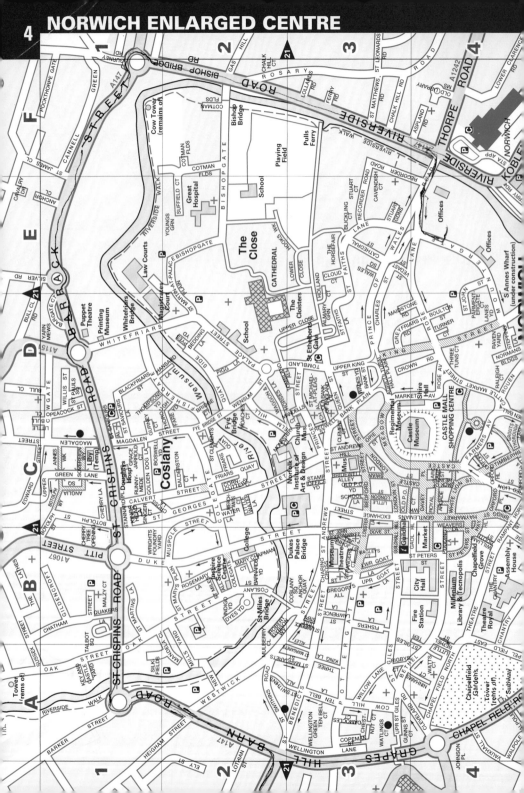

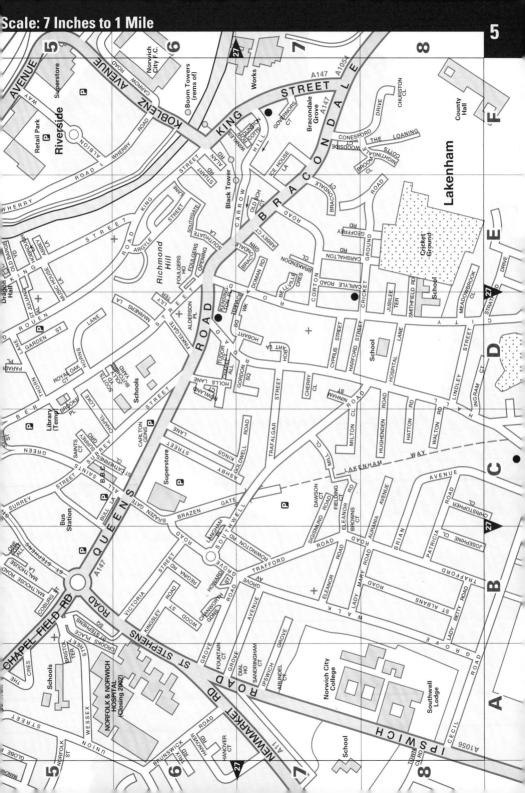

A   B   C   D

Hoveton

Wroxham

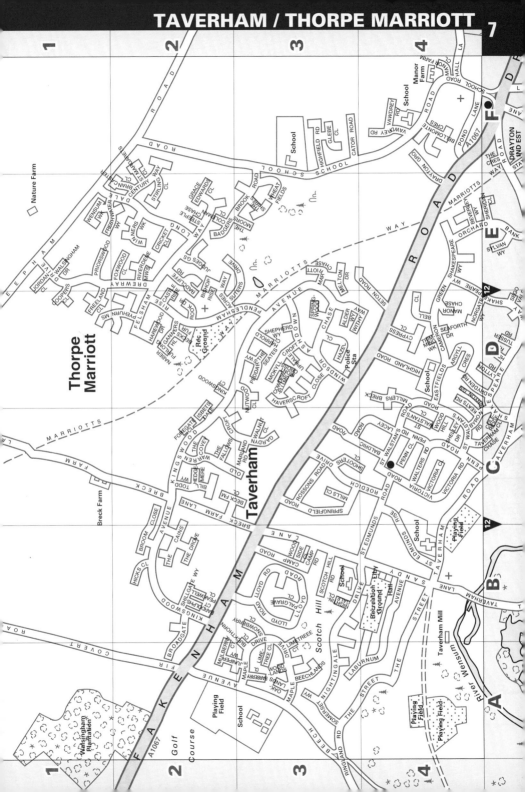

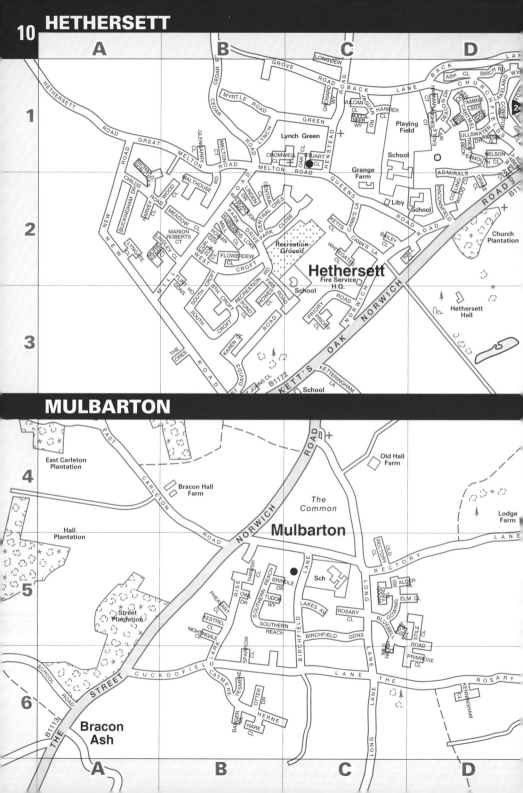

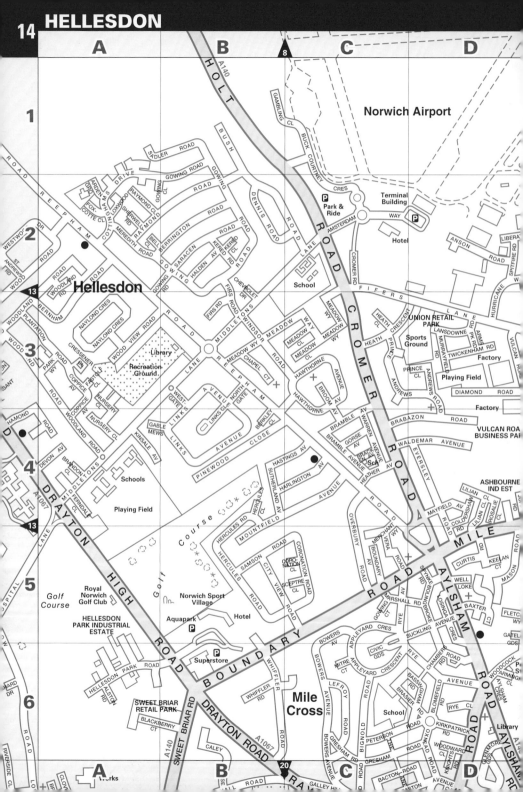

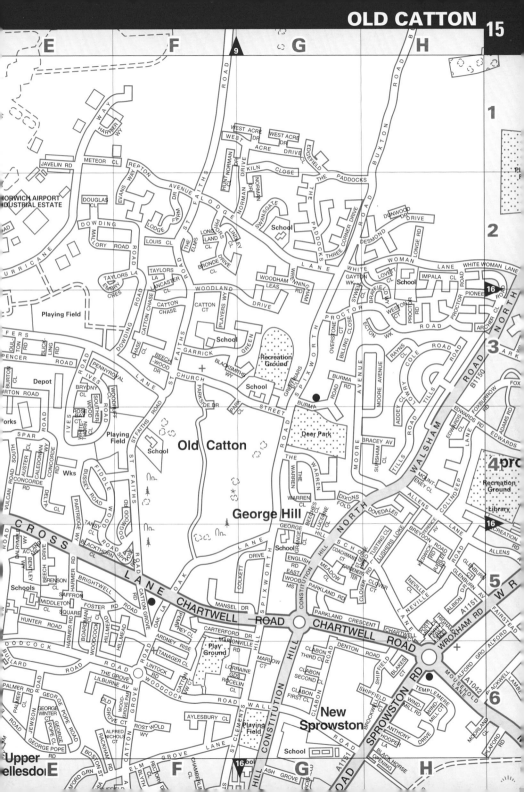

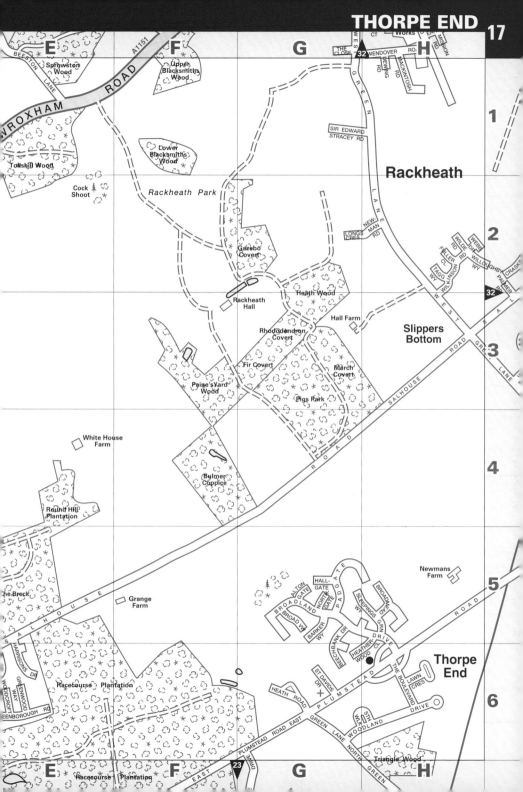

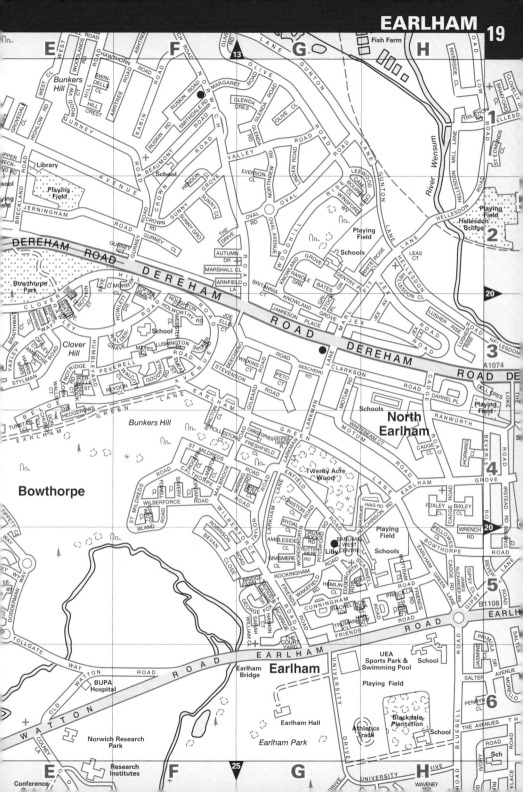

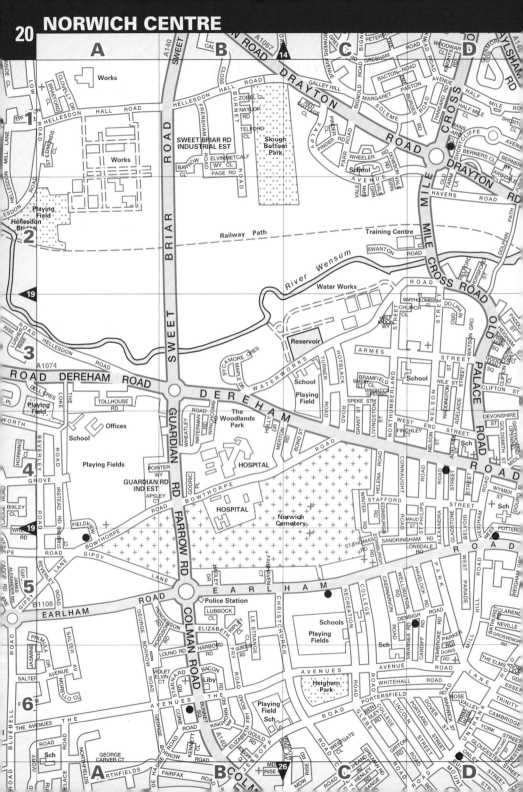

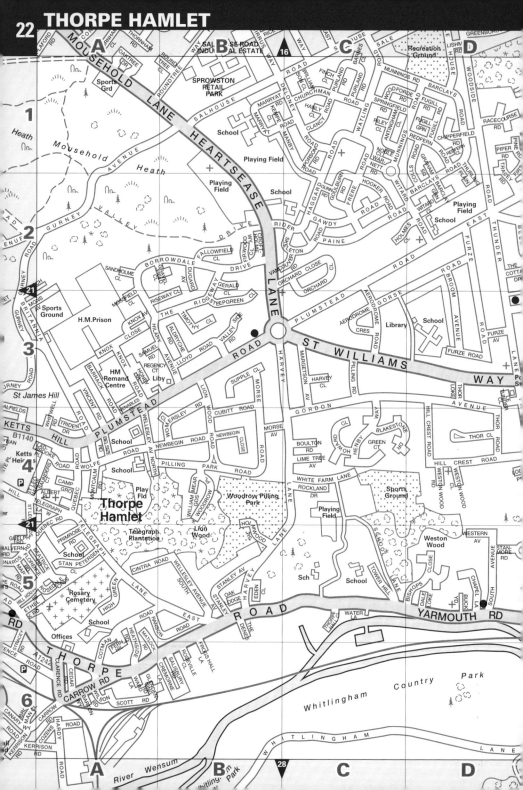

E   F   23   NORWIC   G   H

Hlingham
Marsh

Old Wood

Whitlingham

Sewage
Works

1

Beech
Plantation

Kirby Marsh

2

Red Barn
Plantation

3

Jubilee
Plantation

4

Timber
Hill

James
Spinney

Hill Farm

Kirby Bedon

5

Blyth's
Grove

EAST HILL LANE   EASTHILL LANE

KIRBY   ROAD

TRUMPERY LANE

LODDON

Cockshoot
Plantation

SALLOW LANE

6

A146

ROAD

E   F   G   H

Map grid references A, B, C, D (columns) and 1–6 (rows).

Keswick

Intwood

Lower East Carleton

Swardeston

Labels visible on the map:

- TAYLOR
- AVEN
- DR
- CL
- WOOD GATE
- SIDELL CL
- CLOSE
- MEADWAY
- QUEBEC CL
- Meadow Farm
- INTWOOD
- TUNGATE CRES
- Shingleford Hall
- Moat
- ROAD LOW
- 25
- Eaton Common
- Fir Hill
- Intwood Carr
- ROAD LOW
- Hall Farm
- NORWICH
- A47
- ROAD
- Little Wood
- SOUTHERN
- Big Wood
- ROAD
- ROAD
- Intwood Hall
- Lilac Plantation
- INTWOOD
- Keswick Hall
- KESWICK
- HALL
- COLLEGE LA
- ELLIS GDS
- BISHOP PELHAM CT
- MULBARTON ROAD
- Foxburrow Plantation
- Breck Plantation
- Playing Field
- BRIDLE LA
- Spruce's Plantation
- LANE
- BY-PASS
- INTWOOD LANE
- Swardeston Common
- THE COMMON
- ROAD
- LANE
- Valley Farm
- School
- HILLSIDE CL
- SHORT LA
- MANGREEN
- LANE
- Pear Head Plantation
- Sewage Works
- THE COMMON
- MAIN
- Swardeston
- Swardeston Hall Farm
- WOOD LANE
- CAVELL CLOSE
- Gowthorpe Manor
- B1113
- NORWICH LANE
- CAVELL LANE

E   F   G   H

Lakenham Common

Harford Bridge

B1113

Norfolk Cycle Way

MULBARTON

IPSWICH ROAD

A140 OLD

26

River Yare

Chapel Hill

A47 BY-PASS

1

Superstore

P

Markshall

2

Harford Farm

SOUTHERN

MARKSHALL ROAD

Norfolk Cycle Way

ROAD

Markshall Farm

IPSWICH

NORWICH

MARKSHALL

River Taz

3

Caistor
St Edmund

Old Hall Farm

VENTA
ROMAN TOWN

4

MANGREEN

Mangreen Hall

MANGREEN

Mangreen Hall Farm

Dunston Hills

IPSWICH ROAD

Sewage Works

STOKE ROAD

NORWICH RD

5

Golf Course

Dunston Common

6

Dunston

A140 IPSWICH ROAD

Diane's Wood

E   F   G   H

Rackheath

Slippers Bottom

RACKHEATH INDUSTRIAL ESTATE

SALHOUSE

Recreation Ground

Village Hall

School

Heath Wood

Hall Farm

Rhododendron Covert

March Covert

Bigs Park

Old H. Farm

Salhouse

Little
Plumstead

A **B** **C** **D**

1

Little
Plumstead

2

Blofield
Corner

Plumstead
Green

Manor
Farm

SALHOUSE

The
White House
Farm

3

COPEMAN RD

Sch

LITTLE PLUMSTEAD
HOSPITAL

Home
Farm

Sewage
Works

Big Woo

4

Witton Run

Great
Plumstead

School

Witton

5

SMEE

WITTON

A.47

6

A **B** **C** **D**

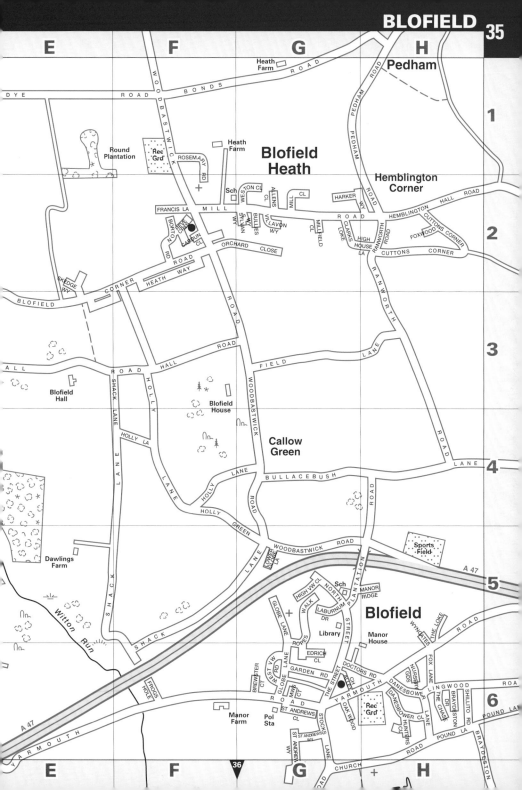

Blofield Heath

Pedham

Hemblington Corner

Round Plantation

Heath Farm

Heath Farm

Blofield Hall

Blofield House

Callow Green

Dawlings Farm

Witton Run

Sports Field

Blofield

Manor House

Library

Manor Farm

Pol Sta

A B C D

1

2

3

4

5

6

B1332

BUNGAY ROAD NORWICH

THE RAMBLERS

HIGHLAND

AISTOR LANE

Old Manor Farm

The Manor Farm

Reservoir Plantation

Poringland Wood

School

Playing Field

OAKLANDS

OAKLANDS

HIGH GROVE CT

GREENACRES DR

CLEARVIEW DR

OAK CROFT

PIGOT

FOX LANE

FOX ROAD

Manor House

Framingham Pigot

THE STREET

SPUR LANE

BEECH WALK

Forty Acre Plantation

School

Radar Station

Radio Station

BIRBECK CL

PINE LORD

STOKE ROAD

THE RIDINGS

BOUNDARY WY

HILLSIDE

OLD MILL RD

MILL RD

ROAD

THE

LONG

TULIP TREE DR

ROMANY WK

CAWSTONS

OAK AV

SUNNYSIDE AV

SPRUCE CRES

HEATH

LOKE

THE FOOTPATH

OVERTONS WY

MULBERRY CL

DEVLIN

BLACKTHORN

HORNBEAM DR

CROMES OAK CL

WINDMILL CL

DRIVE

SPRINGFIELDS

STREET

Framingham Earl

MEADOW

FITZGERA

RIGBY CL

JOHN DREWRY

ALSTON CL

ST ANNES

ST MARYS RD

ST SAINTS

ALL

Sch

HARLESTY

PAGE

ELIZABETH DR

PHILIP DR

HADEN

MALTEN CL

ST ANDREWS

ST MARYS ROAD

ROSEBERY AV

ROAD

FALLOWFIELD

BLIGH CL

IVY CL

UPGATE

BURGATE LA

TANKWELL

BRAMBLE CL

WHITE HOUSE GDNS

WY

Cemetery

GREEN FALL

RECTORY ROAD

Poringland

Rec Grd

Upper Stoke

CAROL CL

PORINGLAND

Bungalow Farm

Brickle Wood

Long Plantation

Dormer House

CARR LANE

SHOTESHAM

LEAFOAK LA

OAK WEST VW

SAXONFIELDS

CHURCH CL

CHURCH LANE

ALDER CL

MEADOW VW

BAYNES

BELLAMY WY

CRITOPH CL

FORGE CL

BUNGAY

WASH LANE

ROAD

B1332

GLENN RD

BARRI CL

HOWE LANE

Abbots Plantation

Wymondham

A - Z INDEX TO STREETS
with Postcodes

The Index includes some names for which there is insufficient space on the maps. These names are indicated by an * and are followed by the nearest joining thoroughfare.

Broadgate NR8 7 A2
Broadhurst Rd NR4 26 D4
Broadland Dr NR13 17 G5
Broadmead Grn NR13 17 H5
Broadsman Cl NR1 21 H6
Brockwell Ct NR3 15 H6
Bronde Cl NR6 15 F2
Brooke Pl NR1 5 C5
Brooks Rd NR10 3 C5
Broom Av,
 Hellesdon NR6 14 C3
Broom Av,
 Thorpe St Andrew
 NR7 22 D2
Broom Cl,
 Bracondale NR1 5 F7
Broom Cl,
 Taverham NR8 7 B2
Broom La NR9 11 A3
Browick Rd NR18 38 D3
Browns Ct NR1 5 C5
Brundall Gdns NR13 36 A4
Brundall Rd NR13 36 E3
Brunswick Rd NR2 21 E6
Bryony Cl NR6 15 E3
Buccaneer Way NR9 10 C1
Buck Courtney Cres
 NR6 14 C1
Buck Yd NR7 22 D5
Buckingham Dr NR9 10 A2
Buckingham Rd NR4 26 B1
Buckland Rise NR4 26 B4
Buckthorn Cl NR8 7 A3
Bull Cl NR3 21 G3
Bull Cl NR3 21 F3
Bull La NR1 5 C5
Bullace Rd NR5 18 D1
Bullacebush La NR13 35 G4
Bullard Rd NR3 15 E6
Bullies Way NR13 35 G2
Bullock Hill NR10 8 B4
Bumpestede Ct NR5 19 E2
Bungalow La NR7 23 F5
Bungay Rd NR14 37 A1
Bunkel Rd NR13 32 A3
Bunnet Sq NR4 20 B6
Bunyan Cl NR7 23 H2
Bure Cl NR12 6 B2
Bure Rd NR12 6 B3
Burgate La NR14 37 D4
Burges Rd NR3 20 C1
Burhill Cl NR4 26 B4
Burma Ct NR3 21 F3
Burma Rd NR6 15 G3
Burnet Rd NR3 20 B1
Burnthouse La NR9 24 A3
Burton Cl NR6 15 E3
Burton Dr NR13 32 C6
Burton Rd NR6 15 E3
Bury St NR2 26 D1
Bush Rd NR6 14 B1
Bussey Rd NR6 15 E4
Buttercup Way NR5 19 E5
Buttermere Rd NR5 19 G5
Buxton Cl NR9 11 B2
Buxton Rd,
 Horstead NR12 3 A2
Buxton Rd,
 Norwich NR3 21 F2
Buxton Rd,
 Spixworth NR10 9 F1
Byfield Cl NR3 21 E1
Byron Rd NR8 7 C4

Cadge Cl NR5 19 H4
Cadge Rd NR5 19 H3,5
Caernarvon Rd NR2 20 C5
Caistor La NR14 37 A2
Caledonian Way NR6 15 E4
Caley Cl NR3 14 B6
Calf La NR10 8 C4
Calthorpe Rd NR5 19 F4
Calvert St NR3 4 C1
Camberley Rd NR4 26 C2
Cambourne Cl NR5 19 G2
Cambridge St NR2 20 D6
Cameron Grn NR8 7 D4
Camp Gro NR1 22 A4
Camp Rd NR8 7 B3
Campbell Ct NR3 21 H2
Canary Way NR1 21 H6
Canfor Rd NR13 32 B5
Cannell Grn NR1 4 F1
Cannerby La NR7 16 A5
Canns La NR9 10 C2
Canns Yd*,
 Queen St NR18 38 C3
Cantley La NR4 25 F6

Capps Rd NR3 21 G1
Cardiff Rd NR2 20 D6
Cardinal Cl NR9 11 C1
Cardun Cl NR13 35 F2
Carleton Cl,
 Norwich NR7 16 B5
Carleton Cl,
 Wymondham NR18 38 C1
Carleton Rd NR7 16 B5
Carlton Gdns NR1 5 C6
Carlton Gdns NR1 5 C6
Carlyle Rd NR1 5 E7
Carnoustie NR4 26 C3
Carol Cl NR14 37 A3
Caroline Ct NR4 26 B1
Carr La NR14 37 C5
Carrow Hill NR1 5 E7
Carrow Rd NR1 5 F6
Carrs Hill Cl NR8 13 E5
Carshalton Rd NR1 5 E7
Carter Rd NR8 13 E1
Carterford Dr NR3 16 F5
Cartmel NR9 10 D1
Castle Mdw NR1 4 C4
Castle Rise NR8 7 D2
Castle St, Norwich NR2 4 C4
Castle St,
 Wroxham NR12 6 A5
Castleton Cl NR5 18 D3
Caston Rd NR7 23 E2
Cathedral St NR1 4 E3
Catmere Herne NR14 10 B6
Cator Rd NR8 7 F3
Cattle Market St NR1 4 D4
Catton Chase NR6 15 F3
Catton Cl NR6 15 F3
Catton Grove Rd NR3 15 F5
Catton View Ct NR3 15 F6
Causeway Cl NR2 20 D3
Cavalier Cl NR7 23 G4
Cavalry Ride NR3 21 F3
Cavell Cl NR14 30 C6
Cavell Rd NR1 27 G3
Cavendish Ct NR1 4 E3
Cavick Rd NR18 38 A4
Cawstons Mdw NR14 37 C3
Cecil Rd NR1 5 A8
Cedar Av NR10 9 G3
Cedar Ct NR18 38 E1
Cedar Rd,
 Hethersett NR9 10 B1
Cedar Rd,
 Norwich NR1 22 A6
Cedar Way NR13 36 C3
Cemetery La NR18 38 C4
Central Av NR7 23 G4
Central Cl NR9 10 B2
Central Cres NR9 10 B2
Century Way NR8 7 E2
Cere Rd NR7 16 C5
Chalk Hill Ct NR1 4 F2
Chalk Hill Rd NR1 4 F3
Chamberlin Cl NR3 21 F1
Chamberlin Rd NR3 21 F1
Chambers Rd NR3 14 D6
Chancel Cl NR13 36 B3
Chancellors Dr NR4 25 F1
Chandlers Cl*,
 Chandlers Hill NR18 38 C3
Chandlers Cl NR4 26 B5
Chandlers Hill NR18 38 C3
Chantry Rd NR2 4 B4
Chapel All NR1 5 D6
Chapel Break Rd NR5 18 C3
Chapel Ct NR6 14 B3
Chapel Field Rd NR2 4 A4
Chapel Fld East NR2 4 A4
Chapel Fld North NR2 4 A4
Chapel La,
 Coltishall NR12 3 C1
Chapel La,
 Norwich NR7 22 D5
Chapel La,
 Wymondham NR18 38 A1
Chapel Loke,
 Norwich NR1 5 C5
Chapel Loke,
 Salhouse NR13 33 G1
Chargrove Fld NR7 23 G3
Charing Cross NR2 4 B3
Charles Av NR7 23 E3
Charles Cl NR12 6 A4
Charles Ct NR12 6 B5
Charles Jewson Ct*,
 Mile Cross Rd NR3 20 D1
Charles St NR1 4 D3
Charles Watling Way
 NR5 18 D2
Charolais Cl NR14 28 B3

Chartwell Ct NR7 15 H5
Chartwell Rd NR3 15 F5
Chase Cl NR6 15 F3
Chatham St NR3 4 B1
Chenery Dr NR7 16 B3
Cherry Cl NR1 5 D7
Cherry La NR3 4 C1
Cherry Tree Opening
 NR3 4 B1
Chester Pl NR2 21 E5
Chester St NR2 26 D1
Chestnut Av NR10 9 G2
Chestnut Cl NR5 18 D1
Chestnut Cl NR2 4 A3
Chestnut Hill NR4 26 A4
Chevrolet Dr NR6 14 B2
Cheyham Mount NR4 26 B4
Cheyney Av NR13 33 G3
Childs Rd NR9 10 A2
Chipperfield Rd NR7 22 D1
Chittock Cl NR10 9 G4
Choseley Ct NR18 38 C3
Christchurch Ct NR2 26 D2
Christchurch Rd NR2 20 B5
Christine Rd NR10 9 G4
Christopher Cl NR1 27 F2
Christopher Ct NR5 19 G4
Church Alley,
 Blofield NR13 35 G6
Church Alley,
 Norwich NR3 4 C3
Church Av NR4 26 C2
Church Av East NR2 26 D1
Church Cl,
 Coltishall NR12 3 B2
Church Cl,
 Horstead NR12 3 A2
Church Cl,
 Norwich NR2 20 C3
Church Cl,
 Poringland NR14 37 C5
Church Grn NR7 16 B3
Church La,
 Brundall NR13 36 E2
Church La, Easton NR9 11 A1
Church La, Eaton NR4 26 A4
Church La,
 Poringland NR14 37 C5
Church La,
 Spixworth NR10 8 D3
Church La,
 Sprowston NR7 16 B3
Church La,
 Wroxham NR12 6 A4
Church Rd,
 Blofield NR13 36 E2
Church Rd,
 Great Plumstead
 NR13 34 A5
Church Rd NR12 6 B3
Church St,
 Coltishall NR12 3 B2
Church St,
 Horsham St Faith
 NR10 8 A4
Church St,
 Old Catton NR6 15 F3
Church St,
 Wymondham NR18 38 B3
Church View Ct NR7 16 A3
Churchfield NR4 25 H5
Churchfields NR9 10 D1
Churchill Rd NR3 21 F2
Churchman Rd NR7 22 C1
Churston Cl NR1 5 F8
Cintra Rd NR1 22 A5
Cirrus Way NR7 16 B6
City Rd NR1 27 G2
City View Rd NR6 14 B5
Civic Gdns NR3 14 C6
Clabon First Cl NR3 15 G6
Clabon Rd NR3 15 G6
Clabon Second Cl
 NR3 15 G6
Clabon Third Cl NR3 15 G6
Claire Cl NR18 38 D2
Clancy Rd NR7 22 C1
Clare Cl NR3 21 F2
Claremont Rd NR4 26 C2
Clarence Rd NR1 22 A6
Clarendon Rd NR2 20 D5
Clarendon Steps*,
 Bathurst Rd NR2 20 D5
Clarke Rd NR3 21 F2
Clarks Loke NR13 35 G2
Clarkson Rd NR5 19 G3
Clearview Dr NR14 37 B3
Clement Ct NR2 4 C3

Clements Way NR13 36 B3
Cleveland Rd NR2 4 A4
Cleves Way NR8 12 C5
Clifton Cl NR2 20 D3
Clifton Rd NR18 38 C1
Clifton St NR2 20 D3
Cloud Ct NR1 4 E3
Clovelly Dr NR6 10 A1
Clover Ct NR7 15 H5
Clover Hill Rd NR5 19 E3
Clover Rd NR7 15 G5
Coach & Horses Row
 NR2 5 A5
Coachmans Ct NR7 15 G5
Cobham Way NR7 16 B6
Coburg St NR2 5 B5
Cock St NR18 38 B2
Coke Rd NR1 27 G3
Coldershaw Rd NR6 14 D4
Coleburn Rd NR1 27 F5
Colegate NR3 4 C2
Coleman Cl NR8 7 E2
Coleridge Ct NR8 12 B1
Colindeep La NR7 15 H4
Colkett Dr NR6 15 G5
College La NR4 30 D3
College Rd NR2 20 C5
Collingwood Cl NR9 10 D2
Collins Ct NR3 21 F1
Colls Rd NR7 22 D2
Colman Rd NR4 20 B5
Colney Dr NR4 25 H4
Colney La,
 Colney NR4 19 E6
Colney La,
 Hethersett NR9 24 B6
Coltishall La NR10 8 B4
Columbine Rd NR10 3 C6
Common La NR7 23 E5
Commonwealth Way
 NR7 23 G2
Concorde Rd NR6 15 E4
Conesford Dr NR1 5 F7
Coniston Cl,
 Hethersett NR9 10 D1
Coniston Cl,
 Norwich NR5 19 G4
Connaught Rd NR2 20 C4
Constable Rd NR4 26 D4
Constable Ter NR4 25 G1
Constitution Hill
 NR3,6 21 G1
Convent Rd NR2 21 E5
Conyers NR18 38 D1
Cooke Cl NR5 18 C3
Coopers Cl NR8 7 D1
Coopers La NR1 27 F5
Copeman Rd NR13 34 C3
Copeman St NR2 4 A3
Copper Smith Way
 NR18 38 F2
Coppice Av NR6 14 A3
Corbett Av NR7 16 A6
Corie Rd NR4 20 B6
Corncutters Cl NR3 4 C2
Corner La NR10 3 C6
Cornwallis Ct NR5 19 E3
Coronation Cl NR6 14 B5
Coronation Rd NR6 14 C5
Corton Rd NR1 5 D7
Coslany Sq NR3 4 B3
Coslany St NR3 4 B2
Costessey La NR8 12 C2
Cotman Flds NR1 5 D6
Cotman Rd NR1 22 A6
Cottinghams Dr NR6 14 A2
Coughtrey Cl NR7 16 A4
Courtenay Cl NR5 18 D3
Cow Hill NR2 4 A3
Cowdewell Mews NR8 7 D3
Cowgate NR3 4 C1
Cowslip Cl NR14 10 C5
Cozens Cl NR1 22 A6
Cozens-Hardy Rd NR7 16 A4
Crabapple Cl NR18 38 E3
Cranage Rd NR1 27 G4
Cranleigh Rise NR4 26 B3
Cranley Rd NR7 23 H3
Cranwell Gdns NR14 37 D4
Cranworth Gdns NR1 5 B6
Craske Dr NR13 32 B5
Craske Mews NR5 18 C3
Creance Rd NR7 16 B5
Cremorne La NR1 22 B6
Cressener St NR1 14 A3
Cresswell Cl NR5 19 F4
Cricket Cl NR8 7 E2

Cricket Ground Rd NR1 5 D
Cricketfield Vw NR13 36 E
Cringleford Chase
 NR4 25 G
Critoph Cl NR14 37 D
Croftholme Way NR1 22 B
Crome Rd NR3 21 G
Cromer Rd,
 Horsham St Faith
 NR10 8 A
Cromer Rd,
 Norwich NR6 14 C
Cromes Oak Cl NR14 37 C
Cromwell Cl NR9 10 B
Cromwell Rd NR7 16 A
Crooks Pl NR1 5 C
Cross Keys Cl NR10 8 B
Cross La NR3 4 C
Crostwick La NR10 9 G
Crowes Loke NR13 34 C
Crown Rd,
 Horsham St Faith
 NR10 8 B
Crown Rd,
 New Costessey NR5 19 F
Crown Rd,
 Norwich NR1 4 C
Crummock Rd NR6 19 G
Cubitt Rd NR1 22 B
Cuckoo La NR13 36 F
Cuckoofield La NR14 10 A
Cucumber La NR13 36 B
Culverin Cl NR7 23 C
Cunningham Rd NR5 19 C
Cursons Mews NR18 38 E
Curtis Rd NR6 14 D
Curzon Cl NR9 10 E
Cutler Way NR5 18 C
Cuttons Corner NR13 35 H
Cypress Cl NR8 7 D
Cyprus St NR1 5 D
Cyril Rd NR7 23 E

Dacre Cl NR4 26 A
Dakenham Cl NR13 32 D
Dakin Rd NR3 21 F
Dalber Cl NR13 23 H
Dale Loke NR7 22 D
Dales Pl NR7 23 E
Dalrymple Way NR6 15 E
Damgate Cl NR18 38 E
Damgate St NR18 38 C
Damocles Ct NR2 4 A
Danby Cl NR4 26 D
Danesbower Cl NR13 35 H
Danesbower La NR13 35 H
Daniels Rd NR2 26 D
Darrel Pl NR5 19 H
Davey Pl NR2 4 C
Davidson Cl NR7 23 E
Davidson Rd NR7 23 E
Dawson Ct NR1 5 C
De Caux Rd NR3 21 G
De Hague Rd NR4 26 A
Deacon Dr NR9 10 D
Deborough Way NR13 23 H
Deepdale NR13 36 C
Delane Rd NR8 13 C
Dell Cres NR5 19 H
Dell Loke NR5 28 A
Deloney Rd NR7 22 B
Delta Cl NR5 18 E
Denbigh Rd NR2 20 C
Denmark Opening
 NR3 21 G
Denmark Rd NR3 21 G
Denmead Cl NR4 26 C
Dennis Rd NR6 14 E
Denton Rd NR3 15 G
Derby St NR2 21 E
Dereham Rd,
 Easton NR9 11 A
Dereham Rd,
 Norwich NR2,5 21 E
Dersley Ct NR5 18 C
Desmond Dr NR6 15 H
Devlin Dr NR14 37 C
Devon Av NR6 14 A
Devon Way NR14 28 E
Devonshire St NR2 20 D
Dewing Rd NR13 32 A
Dial Ho NR1 5 A
Diamond Rd NR6 14 D
Dian Rd NR13 36 E
Dibden Rd NR3 21 G
Dixon Rd NR7 16 A
Dixons Fold NR6 15 G
Dobbs La NR13 32 A

Harvey Cl,
  Norwich NR7 22 C3
Harvey La NR7 22 B3
Harwood Rd NR1 27 F4
Haslips Cl NR2 20 D4
Hassett Cl NR3 21 H3
Hastings Av NR6 14 B4
Hatton Rd NR1 5 C8
Haughs End Rd NR12 6 D5
Hautbois Rd NR12 3 A1
Havant Cl NR4 26 A4
Havelock Rd NR2 20 D5
Havers Rd NR3 20 D2
Haverscroft Cl NR8 7 D3
Hawthorn Rd NR7 9 G4
Hawthorn La NR2 26 D2
Hawthorn Rd NR5 13 E6
Hawthorne Av NR6 14 C3
Hawthorne Cl NR18 38 E1
Hay Hill NR2 4 B4
Haydon Ct*,
  Eleanor Rd NR1 5 C7
Haymarket NR2 4 C4
Hazel Cl, Norwich NR8 7 D3
Hazel Cl,
  Wymondham NR18 38 E3
Hazel Rd NR5 18 D1
Hearne Ct NR5 18 C3
Heartsease La NR7 22 B1
Heath Cl,
  Horsford NR10 3 B6
Heath Cl,
  Norwich NR6 14 C3
Heath Cres NR6 14 C3
Heath Loke NR14 37 B4
Heath Rd,
  Norwich NR3 21 F2
Heath Rd,
  Thorpe End NR13 17 G6
Heath Way NR13 35 F2
Heather Av NR6 14 C4
Heatherwood Cl NR13 17 G6
Heathgate NR3 21 H3
Heathside Rd NR1 22 A5
Hedgemere NR8 7 C2
Heigham Gro NR2 20 D5
Heigham Rd NR2 20 D5
Heigham St NR2 4 A1
Helena Rd NR2 20 C4
Helford St NR2 20 D2
Hellesdon Cl NR5 19 H2
Hellesdon Hall Rd
  NR6 20 A1
Hellesdon Mill La NR6 19 H2
Hellesdon Park Rd
  NR6 14 A6
Hellesdon Rd NR6 19 H2
Hellgate Ct*,
  St Margarets Alley
  NR2 4 A3
Hemblington Hall Rd
  NR13 35 H2
Hemlin Cl NR5 19 G5
Hemmings Cl NR5 19 E3
Hempsted Mews NR5 18 C3
Henby Way NR7 22 C4
Henderson Rd NR4 20 A5
Hendon Cl NR5 19 F2
Henley Rd NR2 26 C1
Henstead Rd NR9 10 C1
Herbert Nursery Cl
  NR8 13 G2
Herbert Robert Glade
  NR18 38 E3
Hercules Cl NR6 14 B4
Hercules Rd NR6 14 B5
Heron Cl NR13 33 G2
Herrick Rd NR8 12 C1
Hethersett La NR4 24 C4
Hethersett Rd NR9 10 A1
Hewitts La NR18 38 C2
Hicks Cl NR8 7 B2
High Grn NR1 22 A5
High House Av NR18 38 E2
High House Cl NR18 38 E1
High House La NR13 35 G2
High St NR12 3 B2
High View Cl NR13 35 G5
Higham Cl NR7 15 H5
Highfield NR13 34 C1
Highfield Av NR13 36 D3
Highfield Cl NR7 23 F4
Highfield Rd NR8 7 F3
Highfields NR5 18 C2
Highgrove Ct NR14 37 B2
Highland NR14 37 A1
Highland Av NR2 26 C1
Highland Cres NR14 28 B3

Highland Rd,
  Norwich NR2 26 C1
Highland Rd,
  Taverham NR8 7 D4
Highlands NR8 12 D5
Highlow Rd NR5 19 E1
Hilary Av NR1 22 A3
Hill Crest NR5 19 E1
Hill Crest Rd NR7 22 D3
Hill Farm Cl NR4 25 H5
Hill House Rd NR1 21 H5
Hill Rd NR5 19 E1
Hill St NR2 26 D1
Hill Top Dr NR8 13 E5
Hillmead NR3 15 E5
Hillside NR14 37 B3
Hillside Av NR3 23 E5
Hillside Cl,
  Norwich NR7 23 E4
Hillside Cl,
  Swardeston NR14 30 C5
Hillside Rd NR7 23 E4
Hilly Plantation NR7 23 E4
Hinshalwood Way NR8 12 D5
Hobart Cl NR18 38 D1
Hobart La NR1 5 D7
Hobart Sq NR1 5 D7
Hobrough La NR1 5 E5
Hockering La NR9 18 A5
Hodgson Rd NR4 20 A6
Hog Bog La NR10 9 F1
Holland Ct NR1 4 D3
Holls La NR1 5 D6
Holly Bank NR7 16 A6
Holly Blue Rd NR18 38 E2
Holly Ct NR18 38 E1
Holly Dr NR2 20 B4
Holly Grn NR13 35 F4
Holly La NR13 35 F3
Holmes Cl NR7 22 C2
Holmesdale Rd NR13 36 A3
Holmwood Rise NR7 22 B5
Holt Rd,
  Horsford NR10 3 B4
Holt Rd, Norwich NR6 14 B1
Holworthy Rd NR5 19 F3
Honey Cl NR1 22 A3
Honeycombe Rd
  NR13 33 F3
Hooker Rd NR7 22 C2
Hooks Walk NR1 4 A3
Hooper La NR3 15 H6
Hopton Cl NR7 23 G2
Hornbeam Cl NR7 16 C5
Hornbeam Dr NR14 37 C5
Horning Cl NR5 19 H4
Horning Rd NR12 6 C2
Hornor Cl NR2 27 E2
Horns La NR1 5 D5
Horsbeck Way NR10 3 B6
Horseshoe Cl NR5 18 C2
Horsford St NR2 20 D2
Hospital La,
  Hellesdon NR6 13 H5
Hospital La,
  Norwich NR1 5 D5
Hospital Rd NR13 34 B3
Hotblack Rd NR2 20 C3
Houghton Cl NR5 19 F3
Howard Cl NR7 22 C4
Howard Mews NR3 21 G1
Howard St NR1 5 B6
Howe La NR14 37 C6
Howell Rd NR3 13 G2
Howes Cl NR9 10 B3
Howlett Dr NR5 19 F3
Hubbard Cl NR18 38 A1
Hubbards Loke NR9 10 B2
Hudson Way NR5 18 C3
Hughenden Rd NR1 5 C8
Hughes Ct NR9 10 D1
Humbleyard NR5 19 E3
Hunt Cl NR6 15 F2
Hunter Rd NR3 15 E5
Hunters Cl NR13 35 H6
Huntingfield Cl NR5 18 D2
Hurd Rd NR4 26 A2
Hurn Rd NR8 13 G2
Hurricane Way NR6 14 D3
Hussabeck Cl NR8 12 C5
Hutchinson Rd NR5 19 G5
Huxley Cl NR1 27 G3
Huxley Rd NR1 27 G3
Hyde Ct NR13 23 H2

Ice House La NR1 5 E7
Ilex Ct NR7 16 C5
Impala Cl NR6 15 H2

Independent Way NR7 23 G3
Indigo Yd NR3 4 B2

INDUSTRIAL & RETAIL:
Abbey Farm
  Commercial Pk NR10 8 A3
Ashbourne Ind Est
  NR6 14 D4
Ayton Rd Ind Est
  NR18 38 D4
Bowthorpe Employment
  Area NR5 18 C2
Bridge Ind Est NR18 38 C4
Castle Mall Shopping
  Centre NR3 4 C4
Drayton Ind Est NR8 12 D1
Festival Retail Pk NR5 11 E1
Frost Ind Pk NR8 13 F1
Guardian Rd Ind Est
  NR5 20 A4
Hellesdon Pk Ind Est
  NR6 14 A5
Norwich Airport Ind Est
  NR6 15 E2
Norwich Bsns Pk NR4 27 F3
Pinelands Ind Site
  NR10 3 B4
Pinetrees Bsns Pk
  NR7 16 C6
Rackheath Ind Est
  NR13 32 A3
Riverside Est NR13 36 D4
Riverside Retail Pk
  NR1 5 F5
St Andrews Bsns Pk
  NR7 23 G4
Salhouse Rd Ind Est
  NR7 16 B6
Sprowston Retail Pk
  NR7 22 B1
Spur Ind Est NR18 38 D3
Stalham Rd Ind Est
  NR12 6 D1
Sweet Briar Rd Ind Est
  NR6 20 B1
Sweet Briar Retail Pk
  NR6 14 A6
Union Retail Pk NR6 14 D3
Vulcan Rd Bsns Pk
  NR6 14 D4
White Lodge Bsns Pk
  NR4 27 E5

Ingram Ct NR1 5 D8
Inman Rd NR7 16 C4
Intwood Rd NR4 25 H6
Ipswich Gro NR1 5 A7
Ipswich Rd NR2,4 5 A8
Ireton Cl NR7 23 G3
Irstead Rd NR5 20 A4
Irving Rd NR4 26 D3
Isbets Dale NR8 7 C2
Ives Rd NR6 15 E3
Ivory Rd NR4 25 H1
Ivy Cl NR14 37 D4
Ivy Rd NR10 9 G3

Jaguar Cl NR9 10 C1
James Alexander Mews
  NR5 19 H5
James Green Cl NR10 9 H3
Jamieson Pl NR5 19 G3
Jarrold Way NR5 18 D2
Jasmine Cl NR4 19 H6
Javelin Rd NR6 15 E1
Jay Gdns NR5 18 C3
Jenny Rd NR10 9 G3
Jerningham Rd NR5 19 E2
Jessopp Cl NR2 20 B6
Jessopp Rd NR2 26 B1
Jewson Rd NR3 15 E6
Jex Av NR5 19 H3
Jex La NR5 19 H3
Jex Rd NR5 19 G3
Joe Ellis Ct NR5 19 F3
John Drewry Cl NR14 37 D3
John Howes Cl NR9 11 B2
Jolly Butchers Yd NR1 5 D6
Jordan Cl,
  Norwich NR5 19 F4
Jordan Cl,
  Taverham NR8 7 E1
Josephine Cl NR1 5 B8
Jubilee Rd NR7 15 H5
Jubilee Ter NR1 5 D8
Judges Dr NR4 26 B2
Judges Gdns NR8 7 E2
Judges Walk NR4 26 B2

Julian Rd NR10 9 G3
Junction Rd NR3 20 D2
Juniper Way NR8 7 A3
Jupiter Rd NR6 14 D4

Kabin Rd NR5 19 F1
Karen Cl NR9 10 B3
Keable Cl NR5 19 H5
Keats Rd NR8 7 C4
Kedleston Dr NR4 25 G6
Keelan Cl NR6 14 D5
Kempe Cl NR7 22 B1
Kendal Cl NR9 10 D1
Kennedy Cl NR9 11 A2
Kennett Cl NR4 20 B6
Kenningham Cl NR14 10 D6
Kensington Pl NR1 5 D6
Kered Cl NR6 14 B2
Kered Rd NR6 14 B2
Kerrison Rd NR1 21 H6
Kerville St NR5 19 E3
Kestrel Cl NR14 10 B5
Kestrel Rd NR6 16 B5
Keswick Cl NR4 25 H6
Keswick Hall Rd NR4 30 C3
Keswick Rd,
  Cringleford NR4 25 G5
Keswick Rd,
  Sprowston NR7 15 H5
Ketteringham La NR9 29 H3
Ketts Av NR18 38 C2
Ketts Cl, Norwich NR9 10 C2
Ketts Cl,
  Wymondham NR18 38 C1
Ketts Hill NR1 21 H4
Ketts Oak NR9 10 B3
Key and Castle Yd NR3 4 A1
Keyes Cl NR1 27 G3
Keyes Rd NR1 27 G2
Keys Dr NR12 6 A5
Kiln Cl NR6 15 G1
Kiln Rd NR10 3 B5
Kimberley St,
  Norwich NR2 21 E6
Kimberley St,
  Wymondham NR18 38 D3
King St NR1 4 D3
Kinghorn Rd NR2 20 B6
Kings Head La NR3 4 C1
Kings La NR1 5 C6
Kings Rd NR12 3 C1
Kingsley Rd NR1 5 B6
Kingston Sq NR4 26 B2
Kingsway NR2 21 E3
Kingswood Av NR8 7 B2
Kingswood Cl NR4 26 B4
Kingswood Ct NR8 7 D2
Kinsale Av NR6 14 A4
Kinver Cl NR4 26 C2
Kirby Rd NR14 28 B3
Kirklands NR8 12 C5
Kirklees NR4 27 E5
Kirkpatrick Rd NR3 14 D6
Knights Rd NR3 20 D1
Knowland Gro NR5 19 G2
Knowsley Rd NR3 21 F2
Knox Av NR1 22 A3
Knox Cl NR1 22 A3
Knox Rd NR1 22 A3
Koblenz Av NR1 4 E4

Laburnum Av NR8 7 A3
Laburnum Cl NR10 3 B4
Laburnum Dr NR13 35 G5
Lacey Rd NR8 7 C4
Lackford Cl NR13 36 C3
Ladbrooke Pl NR1 22 A4
Lady Betty Rd NR1 5 B8
Lady Mary Rd NR1 5 B7
Ladys La NR18 38 A4
Ladysmith Rd NR3 21 G1
Lake View Dr NR13 36 B3
Lakeland Dr NR9 24 A6
Lakeland Way NR9 10 D1
Lakenfields NR1 27 G2
Lakenham Rd NR4 27 E3
Lakenham Way NR1 5 C7
Lakes Av NR14 10 C5
Lambert Rd NR7 16 A6
Lancaster Cl NR6 15 F2
Lanes Yd NR1 4 D4
Langham Grn NR13 36 E2
Langham Pl NR1 5 B6
Langley Cl NR4 25 G5
Langton Cl NR5 19 F4
Lansdowne Rd NR6 14 D3
Larch Cl,
  Little Melton NR9 24 B3

Larch Cl,
  Sprowston NR7 16 C
Lark Rise NR14 10 B
Larkham La NR5 19 G
Latimer Rd NR1 27 F
Laud Cl NR7 23 G
Laundry Cl NR7 23 E
Laundry La,
  Blofield NR13 34 D
Laundry La,
  Sprowston NR7 16 D
Laundry La,
  Thorpe St Andrew
  NR7 23 E
Laurel Dr NR13 36 A
Laurel Gro NR13 36 C
Laurel Rd NR7 23 E
Lavender Cl NR10 3 B
Lavengro Rd NR3 21 H
Lawn Cl NR10 3 C
Lawn Cres NR13 17 H
Lawson Rd NR3 21 F
Layer Cl NR5 18 D
Layson Dr NR13 21 G
Layton Cl NR8 13 F
Le Strange Cl NR2 20 B
Le Terrace*,
  Beatrice Rd NR1 22 A
Le Tunder Cl NR7 22 D
Leafyoak La NR14 37 C
Leas Ct NR6 19 H
Leewood Cres NR5 19 G
Lefroy Rd NR3 14 C
Leicester St NR2 26 D
Leng Cres NR4 26 A
Lenthall Cl NR7 23 G
Leonards St NR3 21 F
Leopold Cl NR4 26 C
Leopold Rd NR2 26 C
Leveson Rd NR7 16 B
Levine Cl NR13 36 A
Liberator Cl NR13 32 B
Liberator Rd NR6 14 D
Libra Ct NR7 16 B
Lilac Cl NR10 3 C
Lilburne Av NR3 15 E
Lilian Cl NR6 14 D
Lilian Rd NR10 9 G
Lily Ter NR1 5 D
Lime Kiln Mews NR3 21 E
Lime Tree Av,
  Costessey NR8 12 D
Lime Tree Av,
  Norwich NR7 22 C
Lime Tree Av,
  Wymondham NR18 38 D
Lime Tree Cl,
  Norwich NR10 3 C
Lime Tree Cl,
  Wymondham NR18 38 E
Lime Tree Rd NR8 26 D
Limetree Cl NR8 7 A
Limetreee Ct NR8 7 A
Linacre Av NR7 16 E
Linacre Cl NR7 16 C
Linalls Dr NR8 12 A
Lincoln St NR2 20 C
Linden Dr NR9 10 B
Linden Rd NR5 19 G
Lindford Dr NR4 26 B
Lindley Cl,
  Hethersett NR9 10 A
Lindley Cl,
  Norwich NR6 15 F
Lindley St NR1 5 D
Lindsay Rd NR7 16 C
Lings Cl NR9 3 C
Lingwood Rd NR13 35 H
Links Av,
  Brundall NR13 36 C
Links Av, Norwich NR6 14 E
Links Cl NR6 14 B
Lintock Rd NR9 15 F
Linton Cl NR7 16 B
Linton Cres NR7 16 B
Lion & Castle Yd NR3 4 C
Lion Wood Rd NR1 22 B
Lishman Rd NR7 16 C
Lisle Rd NR5 18 C
Little Bethel St NR1 4 A
Little Bull Cl NR3 4 C
Little John Rd NR4 27 E
Little La NR1 3 C
Little London St NR2 4 C
Little Melton La NR4 24 C
Little Melton Rd NR4 24 A
Little Water La NR3 4 C
Littlewood La NR12 6 C

ingstone St NR2 20 C4
yd Rd,
Norwich NR1 22 B3
yd Rd,
Taverham NR8 7 B3
oster La NR2 4 B3
cksley Rd NR4 27 E5
ddon Rd NR14 28 B3
dge Breck NR8 13 E1
dge Farm Dr NR6 15 F2
dge La NR6 15 F2
dge Pl NR7 22 D4
llards Rd NR1 4 F3
ndon Rd NR18 38 B4
ndon St NR2 4 C3
ne Barn Rd NR7 16 A6
ng Dale NR8 7 E2
ng John Hill NR1 27 G2
ng La,
Mulbarton NR14 10 C5
ng La, Norwich NR9 11 F4
ng Rd NR14 37 B3
ng Row NR3 21 F2
ngbow Cl NR4 27 E4
ngdell Hills NR15 18 C1
ge Rd NR6 15 H2
ngfields Rd NR7 23 F2
ngland Cl NR6 15 F2
nglands Dr NR18 38 A1
ngmead NR1 27 G2
ngmeadow NR13 36 B3
ngs Cres NR13 32 A5
ngwater La NR5,8 18 C1
nsdale Rd NR13 20 D5
nsdale Rd NR13 32 B6
raine Gdns NR3 15 F6
singa Cres NR3 14 D5
thian St NR2 21 E4
uis Cl NR6 15 F2
und Rd NR4 20 B6
velace Rd NR4 26 A1
vett Cl NR6 15 H2
v Rd,
Drayton NR6,8 13 E1
v Rd,
Great Plumstead
NR13 34 A5
v Rd, Keswick NR4 30 C1
wer Rd,
Salhouse NR13 33 H2
wer Clarence Rd
NR1 1 E3
wer Globe La NR13 35 G5
wer Goat La NR2 4 B3
wer St NR3 33 F2
wry Cole Rd NR6 15 H3
wther Rd NR4 26 D4
xwood NR6 14 A2
obock Cl NR2 20 B5
cas Ct NR13 23 G1
cerne Cl NR6 15 G5
ke Cl NR5 18 D1
sher Rise NR6 19 H3
shers Loke NR7 15 H5
shington Cl NR5 19 F3
hart Rd NR4 26 D4
nch Grn NR9 10 B1
ngate Cl NR9 10 A2
ton Rd NR8 12 C1

ackintosh Rd NR13 32 A4
acks La NR5 12 B1
aden Cl NR18 38 B1
agdalen Rd NR3 21 F2
agdalen St NR3 4 C1
agnay Rd NR8 13 G1
agnolia Cl NR10 3 B4
agpie Rd NR3 21 F3
aid Marian Rd NR4 27 E3
aidens Cl NR13 23 G2
aidstone Rd NR1 4 D3
ain Rd NR4 30 B6
albrook Rd NR5 19 F4
allard Cl,
Brundall NR13 36 E4
allard Cl,
Salhouse NR13 33 G2
allory Rd NR6 15 E2
allow Way NR18 38 E3
altby St NR3 21 H2
alten Cl NR14 37 C5
althouse La NR2 5 B5
althouse Rd,
Hethersett NR9 10 B2
althouse Rd,
Norwich NR5 5 B5
alvern Rd NR1 21 H5

Malzy Ct NR3 4 B1
Manby Rd NR7 22 B1
Manchester Pl NR2 21 E6
Mandela Ct NR3 4 A2
Mandells Ct NR3 4 C2
Mangreen NR14 31 E5
Mangreen La NR14 30 C5
Manor Chase NR8 7 D4
Manor Dr NR10 8 B2
Manor Farm Cl NR8 7 F4
Manor Rd NR10 8 B1
Manor Ridge NR13 35 H5
Mansel Dr NR6 15 F5
Mansfield La NR1 27 F4
Manthorpe Cl NR1 27 G2
Mantle Cl NR7 16 C5
Maple Cl NR18 38 E1
Maple Dr,
Norwich NR2 20 B3
Maple Dr,
Taverham NR8 7 A3
Margaret Cl NR6 13 H3
Margaret Cres NR7 23 E4
Margaret Paston Av
NR3 20 C1
Margaret Rd NR5 19 F1
Margaret Reeve Cl
NR18 38 D2
Margetson Av NR7 22 C3
Marigold Cl NR10 3 B5
Mariners La NR1 5 D6
Marion Cl NR12 6 C2
Marion Mews NR7 16 B4
Marion Rd NR1 21 H5
Marion Roberts Ct
NR9 10 B2
Marionville Rd NR3 15 F5
Marjorie Hind Ct*,
Bethel St NR2 4 A3
Mark Lemmon Cl NR4 26 A6
Market Av NR1 4 D3
Market Pl NR18 38 C3
Market St NR18 38 C3
Markfield La NR10 8 D2
Markshall Rd NR14 31 F3
Marl Pit La NR5 19 G3
Marland Rd NR8 7 C3
Marlborough Ct NR7 16 B4
Marlborough Rd NR3 21 F3
Marlingford Rd,
Bawburgh NR9 11 E4
Marlingford Rd,
Easton NR9 11 A4
Marlingford Way NR9 11 B2
Marlow Cl NR3 15 G6
Marriott Chase NR8 7 E3
Marriott Cl NR2 21 E3
Marriotts Way NR8 7 F4
Marryat Rd NR7 22 B1
Marsh Rd NR12 6 B3
Marshall Cl,
Norwich NR5 19 F2
Marshall Cl,
Spixworth NR10 9 H3
Marshall Rd NR3 14 C5
Marston La NR4 26 B5
Marston Moor NR7 23 G2
Martin Cl NR7 16 B5
Martineau La NR1 5 D7
Marwood Cl NR18 38 B4
Mary Chapman Cl
NR7 23 G4
Mary Chapman Ct
NR3 4 B2
Mason Rd NR3 14 D5
Massingham Rd NR3 21 G1
Matlock Rd NR1 22 A5
Maud St NR2 20 D4
Mayes Cl NR5 19 F3
Mayfield Av NR6 14 D4
Meadow Brown Way
NR18 38 E2
Meadow Cl,
Hellesdon NR7 15 G5
Meadow Cl,
Hethersett NR9 10 B2
Meadow Cl,
New Costessey NR5 13 E6
Meadow Cl,
Norwich NR6 14 C3
Meadow Cl,
Trowse NR14 28 A3
Meadow Dr NR12 6 C4
Meadow La NR7 23 E5
Meadow Rd NR5 13 E6
Meadow Rise Av NR2 20 B6
Meadow Rise Rd NR2 26 C1
Meadow Vale NR5 13 E6

Meadow Vw,
Brundall NR13 36 C3
Meadow Vw,
Poringland NR14 37 C5
Meadow Way,
Horsford NR10 3 C5
Meadow Way,
Norwich NR6 14 B3
Meadowbrook Cl NR1 5 D8
Meadowsweet NR10 3 B6
Meadowsweet Rd
NR18 38 E3
Meadway NR4 25 G6
Medeswell Cl NR13 36 B2
Melrose Rd NR4 26 C2
Melton Cl NR18 38 B1
Melton Cl NR9 10 B1
Melton Dr NR8 7 E3
Melton Gate NR18 38 B2
Melton Rd,
Norwich NR9 10 B1
Melton Rd,
Wymondham NR18 38 B2
Memorial Way NR7 23 H4
Mendham Cl NR1 27 G2
Merchant Way NR6 14 C5
Merchants St NR3 4 C2
Meredith Rd NR6 14 A2
Merlin Av NR7 16 B4
Merlin Cl NR12 6 C2
Merlin Mews NR7 16 B4
Merrow Gdns NR4 26 B4
Merton Rd NR2 20 B4
Metcalf Cl NR3 20 B1
Meteor Cl NR6 15 E1
Mews Ct NR13 35 G6
Middle Rd NR13 34 A4
Middleton Cl NR3 15 E5
Middleton Cres NR5 18 D1
Middleton Cl NR18 38 B3
Middleton St NR18 38 B3
Middletons La NR6 14 A4
Midland St NR2 20 D4
Mile Cross La NR3 14 D5
Mile Cross Rd NR3 20 D2
Mile End Cl NR4 26 C2
Mile End Rd NR4 26 C1
Milestone Cl NR5 18 D1
Mill Cl, Blofield NR13 35 G2
Mill Cl, Hethersett NR9 10 B2
Mill Cl, Norwich NR1 5 C7
Mill Cl,
Poringland NR14 37 B3
Mill Cl, Salhouse NR13 33 F3
Mill Cl NR10 3 C4
Mill Gdns NR10 3 C4
Mill Hill NR13 33 H1
Mill Hill Rd NR2 20 D6
Mill La, Horsford NR10 3 C4
Mill La,
Horsham St Faith
NR10 8 C2
Mill La, Norwich NR3 21 F2
Mill La, Blofield NR13 35 F2
Mill Rd,
Hethersett NR9 10 B3
Mill Rd, Horstead NR12 3 A2
Mill Rd,
Little Melton NR9 24 A3
Mill Rd,
Salhouse NR13 33 F2
Mill St NR10 8 C3
Millcroft NR3 21 F1
Millcroft NR5 18 C2
Millers Breck NR8 7 D4
Millers La NR3 21 F1
Millers Way NR10 3 C5
Millfield Cl NR13 35 G2
Mills Cl NR8 7 C3
Millway NR18 38 C1
Milton Cl NR1 5 C7
Minion Cl NR7 23 G2
Mission Rd NR13 32 B3
Mitchell Ct NR5 18 D3
Mitre Cl NR3 14 C6
Mokyll Cft NR8 7 D3
Monastery Ct NR3 4 C2
Money Dr NR14 28 B3
Mons Av NR1 21 H3
Mont Cross NR8 7 D3
Montcalm Rd NR1 22 A4
Montgomery Cl NR5 18 D3
Montrose Rd NR3 22 G2
Moore Av NR6 15 G4
Moorland Cl NR7 15 H6
Morello Cl NR14 20 A6
Morgan Way NR5 18 D2
Morley St NR3 21 G3

Mornington Rd NR2 26 C1
Morris Cl NR5 19 F2
Morse Av NR1 22 B4
Morse Rd NR1 22 B3
Mossfield Cl NR1 22 A3
Mottram Cl NR5 19 H5
Motum Rd NR5 19 G3
Mount Pleasant NR2 26 D1
Mount Surrey NR18 38 D1
Mounteney Cl NR7 15 H4
Mountergate NR1 4 D4
Mountfield Av NR6 14 B5
Mousehold Av NR3 21 G2
Mousehold La NR7 15 H6
Mousehold St NR3 21 G3
Muck La NR13 32 A2
Mulbarton Rd NR4 30 D3
Mulberry Cl,
Norwich NR2 4 A2
Mulberry Cl,
Poringland NR14 37 B4
Mulberry Cl NR8 7 A2
Munnings Rd NR7 22 C1
Muriel Kenny Ct NR9 10 A2
Muriel Rd NR2 26 C1
Murrayfield Rd NR6 14 D3
Music House La NR1 5 D5
Musketeer Way NR7 23 G4
Muspole St NR3 4 B2
Myrtle Av NR8 12 D5
Myrtle Rd NR9 10 B1
Naber Furlong NR8 7 D2
Naseby Way NR7 23 G3
Nasmith Rd NR4 26 A2
Naylond Cres NR6 14 A3
Naylor Rd NR3 20 B1
Nelonde Dr NR18 38 D1
Nelson Cl NR9 10 D1
Nelson St NR2 25 H1
Nelson St NR2 20 D5
Netherwood Grn NR1 27 G3
Neville Cl NR5 15 H5
Neville Rd NR7 15 H5
Neville St NR2 20 D5
New Mills Yd NR3 4 A2
New Rd,
Bawburgh NR9 18 A5
New Rd,
Hethersett NR9 10 A2
Newark Cl NR7 23 G3
Newbegin Rd NR1 22 B4
Newbegin Rd NR1 22 A4
Newbury Way NR7 23 G3
Newcastle Cl NR7 23 G2
Newfound Dr NR4 25 G4
Newman Rd NR13 17 H2
Newmarket Dr NR4 25 H5
Newmarket Rd,
Cringleford NR4 25 F5
Newmarket Rd,
Norwich NR2 5 A7
Newmarket St NR2 26 D1
Newton Cl,
Norwich NR4 26 D3
Newton Cl,
Trowse NR14 28 A2
Nightingale Cl,
Mulbarton NR14 10 B5
Nightingale Cl,
Taverham NR8 7 B3
Nightingale Cotts NR1 5 F8
Nightingale Dr NR8 7 A3
Nightingale La NR3 21 G3
Nile St NR2 20 D3
Ninham St NR1 5 D7
Ninhams Ct NR2 4 A4
Nobel Cres NR12 6 A4
Noble Cl NR7 22 C1
Norfolk Cl NR4 25 F1
Norfolk St NR2 21 E6
Norfolk Ter NR4 25 G1
Norgate Rd NR4 26 A2
Norgate Way NR8 7 D4
Norman Dr NR6 15 F2
Norman Rd NR3 21 F1
Normans Bldgs NR1 4 D4
Norris Ct*,
Elm Hill NR2 4 C3
North Cage Ct NR1 16 C4
North Gate NR6 14 B3
North Park Av NR4 26 A1
North Park Dr NR4 26 B1
North St NR13 35 G5
North Walsham Rd
NR6,10 15 G5
Northcote Rd NR3 21 G2
Northfield Cl NR18 38 B1

Northfield Gdns NR18 38 B1
Northfield Loke NR18 38 B1
Northfields NR4 20 A6
Northgate NR13 17 G5
Northside NR7 23 H4
Northumberland St
NR2 20 C4
Northview Rd NR5 19 G2
Norton Dr NR4 26 C4
Norvic Dr NR4 26 A3
Norwich Common Rd
NR18 38 F1
Norwich Rd,
Hethersett NR9 10 C3
Norwich Rd,
Horsham St Faith
NR10 8 B4
Norwich Rd,
Horstead NR12 3 A3
Norwich Rd,
Little Plumstead
NR13 33 E6
Norwich Rd,
Mulbarton NR14 10 B5
Norwich Rd,
Norwich NR5 13 F6
Norwich Rd,
Poringland NR14 37 B2
Norwich Rd,
Stoke Holy Cross
NR14 31 H5
Norwich Rd,
Wroxham NR12 6 A5
Norwich Rd,
Wymondham NR18 38 C3
Norwich Southern By-Pass
NR5 18 A2
Notridge Rd NR5 19 E3
Notykin St NR5 19 E3
Nurseries Av NR13 36 D3
Nursery Cl NR6 14 A3
Nursery Gdns NR13 35 H6
Nursery La NR8 12 D5
Nutfield Cl NR4 26 A4
Nutwood Cl NR8 7 C3
Oak Av, Norwich NR7 23 E3
Oak Av,
Poringland NR14 37 C4
Oak Cl, Hethersett NR9 10 C1
Oak Cl, Norwich NR5 18 D1
Oak Croft Dr NR14 37 B3
Oak Gro NR10 3 C6
Oak La NR3,6 15 F5
Oak Lodge NR7 22 B5
Oak St NR3 4 A1
Oak Wood NR13 35 G6
Oakdale Rd NR13 36 C4
Oakfield Cl NR10 3 B5
Oakfields Cl NR4 25 H5
Oakfields Rd NR4 25 H5
Oakhill NR13 36 C3
Oaklands,
Poringland NR14 37 B2
Oaklands,
Taverham NR8 7 A3
Oaklands Dr NR4 25 G3
Oaktree Dr NR7 16 A6
Oakwood Dr NR18 38 E1
Offley Cl NR5 19 E3
Ogden Cl NR18 38 C3
Ogden Ct*,
Ogden Cl NR18 38 C3
Old Bakery Ct NR12 3 B2
Old Bank of England Ct
NR3 4 D3
Old Barge Yd NR1 5 E5
Old Farm La NR3 20 D2
Old Grove Ct NR3 15 E6
Old Hall Cl NR14 28 B3
Old Hall Rd NR4 26 C4
Old Lakenham Hall Dr
NR1 27 G4
Old Library Mews NR1 4 F4
Old Mill Rd NR14 37 B3
Old Norwich Rd NR10 8 B4
Old Palace Rd NR2 20 D3
Old Post Office Ct NR2 4 C3
Old Post Office Yd NR2 4 C3
Old Rectory Cl,
Mulbarton NR14 10 C5
Old Rectory Cl,
Norwich NR7 23 E5
Old School Cl NR1 5 E7
Old Warren NR8 7 C3
Old Watton Rd NR4 19 E6
Olive Cl NR5 19 G1
Olive Cres NR10 3 B4

Street	Ref
Thomas Vere Rd NR7	23 E3
Thompson Rd NR7	23 E2
Thompsons Yd NR3	4 C1
Thor Cl NR7	22 D4
Thor Loke NR7	22 D3
Thor Rd NR7	22 D4
Thorn La NR1	5 D5
Thornham Cl NR7	16 A6
Thornham Rd NR7	16 A6
Thoroughfare Yd NR3	4 C2
Thorpe Av NR7	23 E3
Thorpe Cl NR7	23 E3
Thorpe Hall Cl NR7	22 C5
Thorpe Heights NR1	21 H5
Thorpe Mews NR7	23 E5
Thorpe Rd NR1	5 D5
Three Acre Cl NR12	6 B2
Three Corner Dr NR6	15 G2
Three King La NR2	4 A3
Three Mile La NR5	18 D2
Three Score Rd NR5	18 D5
Three Tuns Ct NR1	4 D4
Thrush Cl NR14	10 B5
Thunder La NR7	22 D2
Thurlby Rd NR5	18 C3
Thurling Plain NR7	22 D1
Thurlow Cl NR5	18 C3
Thurston Rd NR5	18 D3
Tiercel Av NR7	16 B5
Tillet Rd NR3	21 G1
Tillet Rd East NR3	21 G1
Tills Rd NR6	15 H3
Timberhill NR1	4 C4
Timothy Cl NR1	22 B3
Tippett Cl NR5	19 E4
Toftes Pl NR5	19 F2
Tollgate Way NR5	19 E5
Tollhouse Rd NR5	20 A3
Tolye Rd NR5	18 D4
Tombland NR1	4 D3
Tombland All NR1	4 D3
Topcliffe Av NR13	33 F2
Tortoishell Way NR18	38 E2
Tottington Cl NR5	18 D3
Tower Cl NR8	12 A4
Tower Hill NR7	22 C5
Tower Hill Dr NR8	12 A4
Town Cl Rd NR2	27 E1
Town Grn NR18	38 B2
Town House Rd NR8	12 C5
Townsend Ct*, Eleanor Rd NR1	5 C7
Townsend Rd NR4	26 D4
Tracey Rd NR7	22 D1
Trafalgar St NR1	5 C7
Trafford Rd NR1	5 B7
Trafford Walk NR12	6 A5
Trendall Rd NR7	16 C4
Trident Dr NR1	22 A4
Trilithon Cl NR6	19 H1
Trimming Walk NR8	7 D4
Trinity St NR2	20 D6
Trix Rd NR2	27 E1
Trory St NR2	21 E5
Troutbeck NR9	10 D1
Truman Cl, Norwich NR5	19 G5
Truman Cl, Salhouse NR13	32 D3
Trumpery La NR14	29 E6
Tuckswood Centre NR4	27 E4
Tuckswood La NR4	27 E3
Tudor Ct NR1	5 D6
Tudor Way NR14	10 B5
Tulip Tree Dr NR14	37 C3
Tungate Cres NR4	25 H6
Tungate Way NR12	3 A3
Tunstall Cl NR5	19 E4
Tunstead La NR12	6 C1
Tunstead Rd NR12	6 B2
Turner Cl NR18	38 E2
Turner Ct NR1	4 D4
Turner Rd NR2	20 C3
Turnham Grn NR7	23 G2
Tusser Rd NR8	12 C1
Tusting Cl NR7	15 H5
Tuttles La East NR18	38 D1
Tuttles La West NR18	38 A1
Twickenham Rd NR6	14 D3
Two Saints Cl NR12	6 B1
Ullswater Dr NR9	10 D1
Union St NR2	5 A5
University Dr NR4	19 G6
Unthank Rd NR2,4	20 D6
Upgate NR14	37 D4
Uphale NR8	7 D3
Upper Breckland Rd NR5	19 E1
Upper Cl NR1	4 D2
Upper Goat La NR2	4 B3
Upper Green La NR3	4 C2
Upper King St NR1	4 D3
Upper St Giles St NR2	4 A3
Upper St NR13	33 G1
Upper Stafford Av NR5	18 D1
Upton Cl NR4	26 B2
Upton Rd NR4	26 C2
Vale Cl NR10	3 C6
Vale Grn NR3	20 C2
Valley Dr NR1	22 A2
Valley Rd NR5	19 F1
Valley Side Rd NR1	22 B3
Valley View Cres NR5	19 E1
Valleyside NR18	38 D4
Valpy Av NR3	20 C1
Vancouver Rd NR7	22 B2
Vane Cl NR7	23 G4
Varvel Av NR7	16 B5
Varvel Cl NR7	16 B5
Vauxhall St NR2	4 A4
Vawdrey Rd NR8	7 F4
Venables Cl NR1	22 A4
Vera Cl NR13	32 C6
Vera Rd NR6	14 C5
Vere Rd NR13	32 B6
Vetch Cl NR18	38 E3
Vicar St NR18	38 B3
Vicarage Cl, Costessey NR8	12 D4
Vicarage Cl, Norwich NR5	19 G5
Vicarage La NR12	6 D2
Vicarage Rd NR3	21 E1
Victoria Cl NR8	7 C4
Victoria Rd NR8	7 C4
Victoria St NR1	5 B6
Villavon Way NR13	35 G2
Vimy Dr NR18	38 D2
Vimy Ridge NR18	38 D2
Vincent Rd NR1	22 A3
Violet Elvin Ct NR4	20 A6
Violet Rd NR3	21 G1
Virginia Ct NR7	16 B5
Vulcan Cl NR9	10 C1
Vulcan Rd North NR6	14 D3
Vulcan Rd South NR6	15 E4
Waddington St NR2	20 D3
Wades Yd NR2	4 D3
Waggon & Horses La NR3	4 C2
Wakefield Rd NR5	19 G5
Wakehurst Cl NR4	26 B4
Walcott Cl NR5	19 F3
Waldeck Rd NR4	26 C2
Waldemar Av NR8	14 C4
Waldergrave NR5	19 E3
Wales Sq NR1	4 E3
Wall Rd NR3	15 G6
Waller Cl NR8	23 G2
Walnut Cl NR8	7 C3
Walpole Gdns NR2	4 A4
Walpole St NR2	4 A4
Walsingham Dr NR8	7 E1
Walters Rd NR8	7 C4
Walton Rd NR1	5 C8
Ward La NR1	22 A6
Ward Rd NR13	33 G2
Waring Rd NR5	19 G4
Warnett Rd NR1	22 C1
Warren Av NR6	14 C4
Warren Cl, Horsford NR10	3 B6
Warren Cl, Norwich NR6	15 G4
Warren Grn NR13	32 D3
Warwick Dr NR18	38 D1
Warwick St NR2	20 D6
Wash La NR14	37 D5
Water La, Cringleford NR4	25 G4
Water La, Great Plumstead NR13	34 A5
Water La, Norwich NR3	4 C2
Water La, Thorpe St Andrew NR7	22 C5
Waterloo Cl NR10	8 B3
Waterloo Park Av NR3	21 E2
Waterloo Park Cl NR3	21 E2
Waterloo Rd, Horsham St Faith NR10	8 B3
Waterloo Rd, Norwich NR3	21 F3
Waterman Rd NR2	20 B4
Waterworks Rd NR2	20 B3
Watkin Rd NR4	27 E5
Watling Rd NR7	22 C1
Watlings Ct NR2	4 A3
Watson Gro NR2	20 D3
Watton Rd NR4,9	19 E6
Watts Ct NR2	4 A4
Waveney Cl NR12	6 C2
Waveney Dr NR12	6 C2
Waveney Rd NR4	25 H1
Waveney Ter NR4	25 H1
Waveney Way NR12	6 C2
Waverley Rd NR4	26 C3
Weavers Cl NR10	8 B3
Weavers La NR2	4 C4
Webb Dr NR13	32 B5
Webster Cl NR5	19 F3
Well Loke NR3	14 D5
Wellesley Av North NR1	22 A4
Wellesley Av South NR1	22 B5
Wellington Grn NR2	4 A3
Wellington La NR2	4 A3
Wellington Rd NR2	20 C5
Welsford Rd NR4	26 D4
Wendene NR5	18 D4
Wendover Rd NR13	32 A3
Wenman Ct NR5	18 D3
Wensum Cres NR6	15 H5
Wensum St NR3	4 D2
Wensum Valley Cl NR6	13 G5
Wensum Walk NR8	7 E1
Wentworth Grn NR4	26 B3
Wessex St NR1	5 A5
West Acre Dr NR5	15 F1
West Cft NR9	10 B2
West Cl NR5	19 E1
West End NR8	12 A3
West End Av, Brundall NR13	36 A3
West End Av, Costessey NR8	12 A4
West End St NR2	20 C4
West La NR10	8 A4
West Par NR2	20 D5
West Pottergate NR2	20 D5
West Rd NR5	13 E6
West View Rd NR13	35 G6
West Vw NR14	37 C6
Westbourne Rd NR12	3 B1
Western Av NR7	22 D5
Westfield Rd NR13	36 C3
Westgate, Norwich NR6	14 B3
Westgate, Wymondham NR18	38 B2
Westgate Cl NR2	20 C6
Westgate Ct*, Westgate NR18	38 B2
Westlegate NR1	5 C5
Weston Cl NR13	35 G2
Weston Ct NR6	15 H3
Weston Rd NR3	15 E5
Weston Wood Cl NR7	22 D4
Weston Wood Rd NR7	22 D4
Westwick St NR2	4 A2
Westwood Dr NR6	13 H2
Westwood Gdns NR18	38 A1
Whartons La NR18	38 B4
Wheat Flds NR8	7 E3
Wheatacre Cl NR10	3 B6
Wheatley Rd NR2	20 B4
Wheeler Rd NR3	20 C1
Wherry Rd NR1	4 E4
Whiffler Rd NR3	14 B6
White Farm La NR7	22 C4
White Gates NR5	18 C1
White Horse La NR14	27 H5
White House Gdns NR14	22 B4
White Lion Rd NR12	3 D2
White Lion St NR2	4 C4
White Rose Cl NR5	19 H2
White Woman La NR6	15 G2
Whitebeam Ct NR5	19 G4
Whitefriars NR3	4 D1
Whitegates Cl NR9	10 C2
Whitehall Rd NR2	20 C6
Whitehorse St NR18	38 C4
Whitethorn Cl NR6	15 E4
Whiting Rd NR4	27 F4
Whitlingham La NR14	28 A2
Whitwell Rd NR1	22 A4
Wilberforce Rd NR5	19 F4
Wilby Rd NR1	27 F4
Wild Radish Cl NR14	10 C6
Wild Rd NR3	21 F1
Wilde Rd NR13	32 B5
Wilkins Ct NR5	19 G3
Wilkinson Rd NR13	32 B5
Wilks Farm Dr NR7	16 A3
William Booth St NR2	4 B4
William Cl NR18	38 D1
William Frost Way NR5	11 F2
William Mear Gdns NR1	22 B4
William Peck Cl NR10	9 G3
William Peck Rd NR10	9 G3
William White Pl NR1	21 H4
Williamson Cl NR7	22 C1
Willis St NR3	4 D1
Willoughby Way NR13	32 B5
Willow Cl NR18	38 D1
Willow Herb Cl NR18	38 E3
Willow La NR2	4 A3
Wilson Rd NR1	22 A6
Winchcomb Rd NR2	20 B4
Windmill Cl NR14	37 C5
Windmill Ct NR3	15 H6
Windmill La NR8	13 E4
Windmill Rd NR3	15 H6
Windsor Chase NR8	7 D3
Windsor Rd NR6	14 B3
Wingate Way NR2	21 E3
Wingfield Rd NR3	21 E3
Winkles Row NR1	5 F7
Winners Walk NR8	7 E2
Winsford Way NR5	19 G2
Winstanley Rd NR7	23 G3
Winter Rd NR2	20 C4
Witard Cl NR7	22 D2
Witard Rd NR7	22 C2
Withy Way NR8	7 D3
Witton La NR13	34 C3
Wodehouse Cl NR18	38 A1
Wodehouse St NR3	21 G3
Wolfe Rd NR1	22 A4
Wolfson Cl NR4	25 H1
Womersley Cl NR1	22 B4
Womersley Rd NR1	22 B4
Wood Avens Way NR18	38 E3
Wood Cl NR9	10 B2
Wood Grn NR13	32 C4
Wood Hill NR8	7 C4
Wood La NR14	30 B6
Wood St NR1	5 B6
Wood View Ct NR5	19 E1
Wood View Rd NR6	14 A3
Woodbastwick Rd NR13	35 F1
Woodcock Cl NR3	15 E6
Woodcock Rd NR3	15 E6
Woodcroft Cl NR7	17 E6
Woodforde Rd NR7	22 C1
Woodgate NR4	25 G6
Woodgrove Par NR3	15
Woodham Leas NR6	15
Woodhill Rise NR5	19
Woodland Cl NR6	13
Woodland Dr, Norwich NR6	15
Woodland Dr, Thorpe End NR13	17
Woodland Rd NR6	13
Woodlands NR8	7
Woodlands Rd NR5	19
Woodrow Pl NR1	22
Woodruff Cl NR6	15
Woodside Cl NR8	7
Woodside Ct NR1	5
Woodside Rd NR7	16
Woodview Rd NR9	11
Woodward Cl NR3	14
Woodyard Cl NR14	10
Wordsworth Rd NR5	19
Wortham Cl NR5	19
Wren Cl NR4	26
Wrench Rd NR5	19
Wrenningham Rd NR6	15
Wrights Ct*, Elm Hill NR3	4
Wrights Foundry Yd NR3	4
Wroxham Rd, Coltishall NR12	3
Wroxham Rd, Norwich NR7	15
Wroxham Rd, Rackheath NR13	32
Wymer St NR2	20
Wynceby Cl NR7	23
Wyngates NR13	35
Yare Valley Dr NR4	25
Yare Valley Rise NR13	36
Yarmouth Rd, Blofield NR13	35
Yarmouth Rd, Norwich NR7	22
Yarn Mews NR3	4
Yaxley Way NR5	19
Yelverton Cl NR6	13
Yesmere NR14	10
Yew Ct NR7	16
York St NR2	20
Youngs Grn NR1	4
Zobel Cl NR3	20

POSTCODES have been reproduced with the permission of The Post Office. Every care has been taken by Estate Publications but The Post Office cannot be held responsible for any errors or omissions. The outward part of the Postcode which is reproduced in this index will not suffice in identifying a particular address. The list of Postcodes is a copyright work of The Post Office.

Edition 540 C 09.0

For an up-to-date publication list and latest prices visit our web site at

www.estate-publications.co.uk

Use the search facility to find the village, town or city you require.

Local Red Books (selection of)

Ashford & Tenterden	Lancaster & Morecambe
Barnstaple & Ilfracombe	Lincoln
Basildon & Billericay	Macclesfield & Wilmslow
Basingstoke & Andover	Maidstone
Bath & Bradford-upon-Avon	Medway & Gillingham
Bedford	Newport & Chepstow
Brentwood	Northampton
Bromley (London Borough)	Norwich
Burton-upon-Trent & Swadlincote	Nuneaton & Bedworth
Cambridge	Oxford & Abingdon
Chelmsford, Braintree & Maldon	Peterborough
Chester	Plymouth, Saltash & Torpoint
Chesterfield	Reading & Henley-on-Thames
Chichester & Bognor Regis	Redditch & Bromsgrove
Colchester & Clacton	Rugby
Crewe	Salisbury, Amesbury & Wilton
Eastbourne, Bexhill, Seaford & Newhaven	Sevenoaks
Exeter & Exmouth	Southend-on-Sea
Fareham & Gosport	Stafford
Folkestone, Dover, Deal & Romney Marsh	Swindon
Gloucester & Cheltenham	Telford
Gravesend & Dartford	Tunbridge Wells & Tonbridge
Great Yarmouth & Lowestoft	Warwick & Royal Leamington Spa
Hereford	Weston-super-Mare & Clevedon
Ipswich & Felixstowe	Winchester
Kidderminster	Wolverhampton (Sheet Map)
Kingston-upon-Hull	York

Super Red Books

Birmingham (Colour)
Bournemouth
Brighton
Bristol
Cardiff
Coventry
Derby
Edinburgh
Glasgow
Leicester
Nottingham
Portsmouth
Southampton (Colour)
Stoke-on-Trent
Swansea

County Red Books

Bedfordshire	Lincolnshire
Berkshire	Norfolk
Buckinghamshire	Northamptonshire
Cambridgeshire	Nottinghamshire
Cheshire	Oxfordshire
Cornwall	Shropshire
Derbyshire	Somerset
Devon	Staffordshire
Dorset	Suffolk
Essex	Surrey
Gloucestershire	Sussex (East)
Hampshire	Sussex (West)
Herefordshire	Warwickshire
Kent	Wiltshire
Leicestershire & Rutland	Worcestershire

Estate Publications, Bridewell House, Tenterden, Kent, TN30 6EP
Tel: 01580 764225   Fax: 01580 763720

For an up-to-date publication list and latest prices visit our web site at

www.estate-publications.co.uk

Official Tourist Maps also include a Gazetteer to Places of Interest

Official Tourist Maps (England)

1	South East England 1:200,000
101	Kent & East Sussex 1:150,000
102	Sussex & Surrey 1:150,000
103	South East England Leisure Map 1:200,000
104	Sussex 1:150,000
2	Southern England 1:200,000
201	Isle of Wight 1:50,000
3	Wessex 1:200,000
4	Devon & Cornwall 1:200,000
401	Cornwall 1:180,000
402	Devon 1:200,000
5	Greater London (M25 Map) 1:80,000
6	East Anglia 1:200,000
7	Chilterns & Thames Valley 1:200,000
8	Cotswolds, Severn Valley 1:200,000
10	The Shires of Middle England 1:250,000
11	The Mid Shires (Staffs, Shrops, etc.) 1:200,000
13	Yorkshire 1:200,000
14	North West England 1:200,000
141	Isle of Man 1:60,000
15	North Pennines & Lakes 1:200,000
16	Borders of Scotland & England 1:200,000

Official Tourist Maps (Scotland)

16	Borders of Scotland & England 1:200,000
17	Burns Country 1:200,000
18	Heart of Scotland 1:200,000
181	Greater Glasgow 1:150,000
182	Edinburgh & The Lothians 1:150,000
183	Isle of Arran 1:63,360
184	Fife 1:100,000
19	Loch Lomond & Trossachs 1:150,000
191	Argyll, The Isles & Loch Lomond 1:275,000
20	Perthshire, Dundee & Angus 1:150,000
21	Fort William, Ben Nevis, Glen Coe 1:185,000
211	Iona and Mull 1:10,000 / 1:115,000
22	Grampian Highlands 1:185,000
23	Loch Ness, Inverness & Aviemore 1:150,000
24	Skye & Lochalsh 1:130,000
25	Argyll & The Isles 1:200,000
26	Caithness & Sutherland 1:185,000
27	Western Isles 1:125,000
28	Orkney & Shetland 1:128,000
28	Shetland & Orkney 1:128,000
30	Highlands of Scotland 1:275,000

Local Leisure Maps

111	Peak District 1:100,000
12	Snowdonia 1:125,000
131	Yorkshire Dales 1:125,000
132	North Yorkshire Moors 1:125,000
151	Lake District 1:75,000
301	Dorset 1:150,000
403	Dartmoor & South Devon Coast 1:100,000
404	Exmoor & North Devon 1:100,000
802	The Cotswolds 1:110,000

General Maps For The Tourist

	Kent to Cornwall 1:460,000
92	England & Wales 1:650,000
9	Wales 1:250,000
93	Scotland 1:500,000
94	Historic Scotland 1:500,000
95	Scotland (Homelands of the Clans)
99	Great Britain 1:1,100,000
99	Great Britain (Flat) 1:1,100,000
100	British Isles 1:1,100,000

European Leisure Maps

Europe 1:3,100,000
Cross Channel Visitors' Map 1:530,000
France 1:1,000,000
Germany 1:1,000,000
Ireland 1:625,000
Italy 1:1,000,000
Netherlands, Belgium & Luxembourg 1:600,000
Spain & Portugal 1:1,000,000

World Maps

World Map - Political (Folded) 1:29,000,000
World Map - Political (Flat in Tube) 1:29,000,000
World Travel Adventure Map (Folded) 1:29,000,000
World Travel Adventure Map (Flat in Tube) 1:29,000,000

Estate Publications, Bridewell House, Tenterden, Kent, TN30 6EP
Tel: 01580 764225   Fax: 01580 763720